HAWKS

by Sharon Sharth

Content Adviser:
The Zoological Society
of San Diego

Published in the United States of America by The Child's World®
PO Box 326 • Chanhassen, MN 55317-0326
800-599-READ • www.childsworld.com

PHOTO CREDITS

© Alan G. Nelson/Dembinsky Photo Associates: 7
© Anthony Mercieca/Dembinsky Photo Associates: 11
© Chase Swift/Corbis: 26–27
© Dale C. Spartas/Corbis: 13
© Eric and David Hosking/Corbis: 25
© Fritz Polking/Dembinsky Photo Associates: 14
© John Conrad/Corbis: 9
© John Watkins/Frank Lane Picture Agency/Corbis: 19
© PhotoDisc: 5
© Ralph Lee Hopkins/Getty: 29
© Renee Lynn/Corbis: 20–21
© Sharon Cummings/Dembinsky Photo Associates: 16–17
© StockTrek/Getty: cover, 1
© W. Perry Conway/Corbis: 23

ACKNOWLEDGMENTS

The Child's World®: Mary Berendes, Publishing Director;
Katherine Stevenson, Editor

The Design Lab: Kathleen Petelinsek, Design and Page Production

LIBRARY OF CONGRESS CATALOGING-IN-PUBLICATION DATA

Sharth, Sharon.
  Hawks / by Sharon Sharth.
    p. cm. — (New naturebooks)
  Includes bibliographical references and index.
  ISBN 1-59296-640-3 (library bound : alk. paper)
  1. Hawks—Juvenile literature. I. Title. II. Series.
  QL696.F32S47 2006
  598.9'44—dc22   2006001368

Table of Contents

On the cover: Harris's hawks like this one live from the southwestern U.S. all the way to Argentina. They are about two feet (61 cm) long and weigh about two pounds (1 kg).

Meet the Hawk!

Hawks are thought to be one of the most intelligent birds in the world.

A large bird soars across the sky with its wings spread wide. From high above a grassy meadow, it sees a mouse. The bird folds its wings and dives toward the ground. Quickly, it reaches out with its feet and grabs the mouse. What is this flying hunter? It's a hawk!

You might have seen a red-tailed hawk like this one soaring overhead. Red-tails are common all across North America. They are named for the reddish brown feathers on the upper side of their tail.

What Are Hawks?

The word "hawk" comes from *hafoc,* an old English word meaning "to grasp or seize."

Hawks often watch for prey from a resting place called a **perch.** A hawk's perch might be a tree branch, a roof, or a telephone pole.

Hawks are part of a large group of birds called **raptors**. Raptors are **carnivores**, which means that they eat the meat of other animals. Eagles, owls, kites, and vultures are raptors, too. All raptors have a hooked beak and very sharp, curved claws called **talons**. Raptors use their talons to catch, hold, and sometimes kill the animals they eat, called their **prey**.

This ferruginous (fuh-ROO-juh-nuss) hawk is standing on a haystack in the American Midwest. These hawks are large, growing to about 23 inches (58 cm) in length and about 3 pounds (a little over 1 kg) in weight.

How Well Do Hawks See?

A hawk's eyes can't move as much as a person's eyes. To see in different directions, the hawk must move its head.

Some kinds of hawks have eyes that change color as they get older. These hawks are born with grey eyes, which turn yellow in about a year.

Hawks can see eight times better than people. They can also see in color.

Hawks have amazing eyesight. Their large eyes let them see to the front and to either side. Even from far away, a hawk can see what another animal is doing. In fact, a hawk can see a mouse from one mile (a little over 1.5 km) away. That means hawks can spot their prey as if they were looking through binoculars!

Most hawks have bones that stick out above their eyes. These bones act like a baseball cap, helping to keep the sun out of the hawk's eyes when it is hunting.

This northern goshawk is carefully scanning a nearby Colorado field for movement. Short wings and a long tail help northern goshawks turn and dive when flying in forested areas.

Where Do Hawks Live?

Many types of hawks like to make their nests near clearings and open areas where they can see their prey more easily. In cities, they sometimes make their nests near paths or roadways.

Hawks live almost everywhere in the world. In fact, just about the only place you won't find hawks is on the cold continent of Antarctica. Accipiters live in or near thick forests, where their favorite prey (other birds) can be found. Buteos prefer to live near grassy meadows or prairies. Some hawks live on icy mountaintops. Some even make their homes in hot, dry deserts.

This young red-tailed hawk is watching a field from a fence post. Red-tails prefer to live in open areas such as prairies, marshes, and even deserts.

Most hawks live in large areas called **territories**. The territory is where the hawk hunts, sleeps, and nests. Both male and female hawks defend their territories from intruders.

Many North American hawks move south, or **migrate**, when the weather turns cold. They fly in groups to warmer areas. They pump their wings and then glide as the air carries them along. In the spring, these hawks migrate north again to have their babies.

Savannah hawks like this one live mostly in South America. They often wait near grass fires, ready to catch animals running from the flames.

Swainson's hawks are known to migrate in groups of several hundred birds. These hawks migrate from the eastern areas of Canada and the United States down to Central and South America.

15

How Are Baby Hawks Born?

While other birds often use items such as string, grasses, and feathers to make their nests, hawks usually prefer sticks, bark, and leaves.

After a male and a female hawk mate, the female lays up to five eggs in a nest. The parents then take turns sitting on the nest and warming the eggs. While one parent sits on the eggs, the other hunts for food and brings it back to its partner. About one month later, the eggs hatch.

The hawk babies, or *chicks*, are covered with soft, fluffy feathers. Their eyes are wide open. The father hunts for food and brings it to a nearby perch. He calls to the mother, and she flies to him. The mother takes the food back to the nest. She tears it apart for her babies, and they grab the pieces from her beak. After about four weeks, the chicks fly. But they might stay with their parents much longer. Some types of hawks need their parents to teach them how to hunt.

Here you can see an adult Cooper's hawk as it feeds its chicks. Cooper's hawks are about the size of a crow and are named for the famous naturalist, William Cooper.

How Do Hawks Hunt?

A little while after eating, a hawk will cough up the fur, feathers, and bone it cannot digest.

Harris's hawks sometimes hunt in groups. Some of the birds scare the prey out of hiding, and the others attack it.

Hawks hunt during the day, when they can see their prey. Many search for small animals such as squirrels and rabbits. Some hawks even eat foxes! There are hawks that eat snakes, lizards, and frogs. Many hawks eat smaller birds, too.

Hawks often hunt sick and injured animals—they are the easiest to catch. Hawks also eat **carrion**, the meat of dead animals. Hawks will eat just about anything, as long as it's easy to get!

18

This northern goshawk has just caught and killed a kestrel. Both birds are fast flyers, so the goshawk had to take its prey by surprise.

Hawks often surprise their victims and kill them quickly. Some hawks hunt animals on the ground, but most hawks attack their prey from above. Hawks will soar over an area for hours watching for tiny movements. When a hawk spots its prey, it folds its wings close to its body and dives headfirst toward the animal.

Hawks can dive at high speeds— up to 120 mph (193 kph).

Here a Galápagos hawk soars high above a grassy area as it searches for prey. These rare hawks live only on the Galápagos Islands. They eat mostly iguanas, rats, and other birds.

21

When the hawk is close enough to its prey, it stretches its legs forward. The hawk then grabs its prey with its strong feet and kills it by either crushing it or stabbing it with its talons. The hawk then flies to its perch and begins to eat. Some hawks swallow smaller prey, such as mice, whole. Larger prey must be torn into small pieces by the hawk's strong, hooked beak.

Long-tailed hawks from Africa break the necks of their prey.

This northern goshawk is landing on a male pheasant. Can you see how the hawk grasps its prey tightly with its powerful feet?

23

How Do Hawks Stay Safe?

Hawks can live to be 20 years old.

Hawks are often in danger. Raccoons, snakes, and other raptors hunt and eat hawk chicks. Healthy adult hawks are sometimes attacked by owls or other animals. Owls will also attack an adult hawk if it appears to be weak or sick.

To help them hide from enemies, hawks have feathers with markings and colors that help them blend in with their surroundings. Many hawks have brown and gray feathers that match the trees, grasses, and ground where they live. Such protective coloring is called **camouflage**.

This red-backed hawk is hard to see as it perches on a seaside cliff. These hawks live in South America as well as the Falkland Islands.

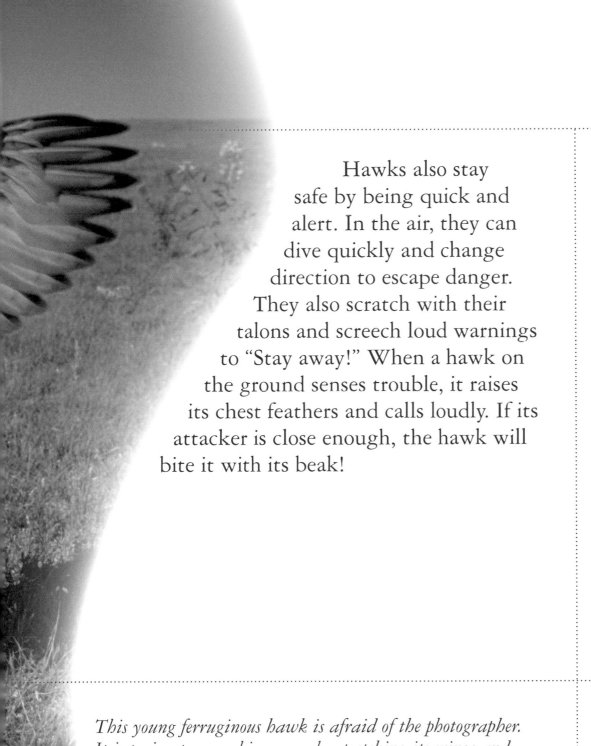

Hawks also stay safe by being quick and alert. In the air, they can dive quickly and change direction to escape danger. They also scratch with their talons and screech loud warnings to "Stay away!" When a hawk on the ground senses trouble, it raises its chest feathers and calls loudly. If its attacker is close enough, the hawk will bite it with its beak!

Hawks can chatter, hiss, screech, scream, and whistle.

This young ferruginous hawk is afraid of the photographer. It is trying to scare him away by stretching its wings and screeching loudly.

How Can You Learn About Hawks?

Like all raptors, hawks are protected in the United States. That means it is illegal to hunt and/or kill them.

To learn more about hawks, listen for warning cries from other birds. When they stop and look toward the sky, there's probably a hawk circling. If you hear a high-pitched chirp and see chipmunks scurrying from an area, a hawk is probably on its way. By watching other animals, you'll know when to look up into the sky. If you see a hawk, try watching it for a while. You'll find much to admire in its strength, beauty, and grace.

This Galápagos hawk is resting on a windy afternoon. He seems to be looking right at you!

Glossary

camouflage (KAM-oo-flazh) Camouflage is colorings or markings that help and animal hide. Many hawks have camouflage.

carnivores (KAR-nih-vorz) Carnivores are animals that eat meat. Hawks are carnivores.

carrion (KAR-ree-un) Carrion is dead or decaying animals. Hawks eat carrion.

digest (DY-jest) To digest food is to break it down into smaller, simpler pieces that the body can use. Hawks spit up fur, feathers, and bones they can't digest.

migrate (MY-grayt) When animals migrate, they move from one location to another. Hawks migrate in search of food or to find a safe place to have their babies.

perch (PURCH) A perch is a place where a bird rests or watches for prey. Most perches are high tree branches.

prey (PRAY) Prey are animals that are hunted and eaten by other animals. Squirrels, mice, and other birds are prey for hawks.

raptors (RAP-turz) Raptors are birds that eat meat. Hawks, owls, and eagles are raptors.

species (SPEE-sheeez) A species is a different kind of an animal. There are more than 40 different species of hawks.

talons (TA-lunz) Talons are the sharp claws of birds of prey. Hawks have talons.

territories (TARE-ih-to-reez) A territory is an area where animals sleep, eat, and have babies. Male and female hawks defend their territories.

To Find Out More

Read It!

Fourie, Denise K. *Hawks, Owls & Other Birds of Prey.* Parsipanny, NJ: Silver Burdett Press, 1995.

Kops, Deborah. *Hawks.* Woodbridge, CT: Blackbirch Press, 2000.

Lynch, Wayne. *Hawks.* Chanhassen, MN: NorthWord Press, 2004.

Ritchie, Rita, Sumner Matteson, John F. McGee (illustrator), and John Hendrickson (photographer). *The Wonder of Hawks.* Milwaukee, WI: Gareth Stevens, 1996.

Schaefer, Lola M., and Gabi Swiatkowska (illustrator). *Arrowhawk.* New York: Henry Holt, 2004.

Wechsler, Doug. *Red-tailed Hawks.* New York: PowerKids Press, 2001.

On the Web

Visit our home page for lots of links about hawks:
http://www.childsworld.com/links

Note to Parents, Teachers, and Librarians: We routinely check our Web links to make sure they're safe, active sites—so encourage your readers to check them out!

31

Index

About the Author

Sharon Sharth was a TV, film, and Broadway stage actor for twenty years before becoming a writer. Today, she writes books and plays and is a regular speaker at schools and libraries. Ms. Sharth also works with an international organization to provide children's books and other support for orphans and vulnerable children in sub-Saharan Africa. She lives in Pasadena, California, with her husband and two dogs.

32